*american bandstand, slices of life
and other poems*

american bandstand, slices of life and
other poems

to my family, present and gone

Acknowledgments:

Grateful thanks to the following anthologies, conferences, and to the editors/websites where the below poems and others first appeared.

- "Pity Party" was published in the March 2016 issue of the *Medical Journal CHEST*, published by Elsevier, Inc. under license from the American College of Chest Physicians.

- The poem "Dirty Laundry" won Honorable Mention and an Honorarium in *The 2015 Robinson Jeffers Tor House Prize for Poetry*. It can be read at: www.torhouse.org

- Fishing for Words" was published in *Borderland Arts* November/December 2014 newsletter and in *Health and Happiness U.P. magazine*. Spring 2015.

- The poem "The Road In" won honorable mention at Save the Wild and can be read at: www.savethewildup.org

- Granger was twice honored by Sigma Tau Delta/International English Honor Society:

In 2014, the collection: *"1924—2014, A Nun's Life"* was the winner of the 90th Anniversary Convention Theme in Savannah, GA. The poems included in the collection were: "The Hand of Fate," "Crooked Red Thread,"

"Walking to Daily Mass," "A True Calling," "The Keeper," and "The Crossing". These poems and others are in a chapbook to be released at later date.

- In 2012: The Isabel Sparks President's Award of First Place in Original Poetry at the Convention in New Orleans, LA. The poems included in the collection, *Slices of Life* were: "Leaving Normal," "Dirty Laundry," "Loose Connections," and "Shall Not Hurt Them."

- Granger's poems were published in: *Celebrations 2007: An Anthology-* Winner of Kathryn M. Sedbury Prize. *Celebrations 2006: An Anthology-*First Place in Non-Rhyming Poetry. *Celebrations 2005: An Anthology-*Winner of Kathryn M. Sedbury Prize.

Special thanks: to Austin Hubbell, who saw these poems in their infancy and showed me what careful revision could do and to Lesley Larkin, my friend and reader. Thank you to my Writing Sisters and to the dear friends I've shared my writing with. To my husband, Keith, who has been there with love and support. Grateful thanks to: Kristine Granger, my daughter, the child beneath my heart without whose wise counsel this book would not be published, to my sweet son, Erik, forever known as the baby in the blueberry patch. Much love to my sister, Lisa, who knows me better than I know myself, and to Judy, my baby-sis. To Rich and Peggy, who cheered me on during poetry readings, and a bucket of love to my grandchildren: Per, Mason, and Carter.

Contents

early lessons

War Baby

I was born to survive,

swam into life two months early.

 The doctors wagered seven months

womb time were not survival odds.

Mama did not listen,

willed me to live.

She tried to keep from crying

when well-meaning folk

      said, "She's pretty."

Mama knew they lied.

No hair, no eyebrows or lashes, no fingernails.

      Just not done.

Hello My Dolly

Nights we fell asleep to her rocking
the least of us. Mama was an orphan
never chosen. Our house bulged
like the "Old Woman Who Lived
in a Shoe." Children came to us

scarred and scared by folks whose job
it was to love them. Mama taught them
to trust again. She'd rock each one
and change the rhythm of their lives.

With a man's hanky, pinned to her apron,
she waged war on noses and drool;
wiped clean doll and baby faces. With
a string of suckers hung from a hook
she taught potty to the toughest holdouts.

Blanket-wrapped, a child, I slept
to the whir of her sewing. She fashioned
velvet dresses, fur-trimmed capes
for my dolls. Mornings she'd hold me
close and whisper *Hello Dolly*.

She found money for a bus to Biloxi
when I was 12, where a cure for asthma
dangled. Four days we traveled, me
bus-sick and Mama bent on my being
whole. I drank spoons of the elixir
until it ate a hole in the tablecloth.

Years later, when my brother was killed,
grief made her sugar climb and gangrene took
her leg. I stayed by her side. She woke
from the coma, whispered, *Hello my Dolly,*
and stayed awhile.

Early Lessons

He taught me to fish, to dig worms and bait a hook. His
hands atop my small we cast out lines in perfect arcs.

The river gulped our offering and bobber's eye stared back.
I prayed for bass or pike, shivered with each minnow's bite.

Lunch was bologna on home-made bread, washed down
with Kool-Aid from a thermos with the taste of tin.

Dragonflies cast spells and black flies hovered. Mosquitoes
droned, bit at ankles, while clouds of gnats gnawed our ears.

River swallows sun and we pack our catch,
four small bass. We head home with new fish stories.

Red Feathers

An axe hangs, a second hand
with its flash of silver edge.
He walks through the skittish flock.
They scatter, sense a fever change,
predict a storm on this clear day,
as I cling to chicken wire.

With a single motion he grabs a copper hen,
pins her to the bloodied stump. The axe falls.
Leaves severed head with one unseeing eye.
He throws the body to the sky.

Red, petal upon petal sprays,
like the scatter of late roses
on a chill November wind.
Screams scorch my throat.
With bloody bird clasped in butcher's hand,
Daddy stills me in his embrace.

I whimper before sleep,
beg to leave the light on.
Beneath tight shut lids, I see

petals upon petals of brilliant red

as rusty feathers spiral.

Friday Night on the Main Drag

We score a great spot in front of Kresge's.
The air is thick with the aroma of hot roasted nuts,
fresh baked doughnuts, the grease luring us in.
I'm twelve; it's Dad's payday.
My two quarters allowance is clutched in my palm.
I'm worn out trying to decide between paper dolls
or a Classic comic. My youngest sister ate hers,
a tin-roof sundae. My brothers have checked out
BB's, baseball cards, and tried to page through girly
magazines at the Bon Ton. They're wary
of combining their wealth. Ownership's
been a problem in the past.
My folks lean against our Chevy,
visit with passersby. A couple
of my cousins run past.
Lumber trucks rumble on through.
Fats Domino's *Blueberry Hill* vibrates
from outside speakers. Old Mrs. Dempsey
stops to talk and I stare at the goiter on her
neck. It's like a prow on a ship. Eventually,
it will choke her to death. Mom swats me
for staring, but not real hard. Pete Wender

wanders over to ask if he can take

my older sister to the dance on Saturday.

I can smell cow shit on his boots. Don't

know how she can stand kissing him. She

does though.

At the Junction

We never lived in town.
Rode a bus to school from
Kindergarten on. On hot autumn
days the bus was ripe with the smells

of cow shit on boots, hormonal
teens, and kids who bathed once
a week. Skittered over black ice
on early winter mornings, huddling
together to keep warm.

Townies called us farmers,
but Daddy's only crop was kids,
his own and those who needed
homes. In the 50's the doors

closed at the Ford Plant, no jobs
to be found. We ate oatmeal for supper
but never felt poor. Dad coaxed a clunker
to life. We rattled to the Drive-In, smuggled

under blankets, to lower the price.
Popcorn from home, everyone in pjs,
hooked on Hollywood until sleep
knocked us out.

Mama's Donation

I learned the mysteries of the rosary
before Mama taught me nursery rhymes.
She explained that God's son
hung on the cross above the altar.

Mama, an orphan, was raised
in a cloistered convent. Each year
we rode the train to visit my nun
grandmothers. She warned me

to behave my best. They thought
I was a delight. They smelled of
candles and strong soap and never
seemed to sweat. They floated upon

the floor in habits of black and white.
Mama loved the nuns and asked me
over and over, "Did I think I could be
a sister and enter in?

She prayed day and night that her
Prayers would be answered. The idea
filled my mind. I questioned, "Was this

what God wanted of me?"

I entered in at fifteen as a novitiate.
Living within Convent walls was
different than going for a visit.
Homesick, I cried each night.

I was taught to not ask "Why"—to obey,
to live by bells, to pray and sing in Latin.
The Sisters could be cruel and harsh,
but shedding tears was not an option.

Some taught with iron fists, with shame
and wielded wooden rulers. The postulants
were told to hold their tongues when parents
came to visit, to not divulge the Order's business.

We worshipped our favorite nuns. On laundry
day, we folded breast binders and wondered
at curves hidden beneath their habits.
They were mysterious, our holy starlets . . .

We took turns reading *The Lives of Saints*,
offered up more difficult things,
imagined seeing visions of the Virgin

Mary, like Saint Bernadette, or of

finding stigmata wounds on our hands
and feet like Sister Rita. On a visit home
I was unsure how to act. Without the Order's
rules enforced, the world was chaotic. I shied

from noise accustomed to meditative silence.
Without my uniform, I felt undressed. Confused,
I was eager to return, envisioned the Nun I'd
become. The outside world beckoned less and I
welcomed Convent walls.

What's Blossoming?

The moon, a silver fist in a black cardboard sky,
spills light across my bed. My eyes travel the
terrain of my body. My toes are ten
soldiers beneath blankets at the end.

Something's altered. I look down at covers
pulled to my chin. Is there an added wrinkle?
I raise the sheet expecting to see the flat
white cotton of my J.C. Penney's undershirt.

No, it's stretched across two boiled eggs that rest
atop a cage of child's ribs. The flat coins that have
marked their centers are rosebuds unfurled. Has
St. Jude answered my prayers?

I'm sixteen and I'm blossoming.

I send a prayer of thanks. I never wanted breasts
to attract the opposite sex. Not in this coven of nuns.
I've wanted to be equal to my peers. To not lag
behind the growth chart as I've done since birth.

I'm normal, I whisper – just to hear the words.

You'd think we daughters of Christ would be above judging each other – would leave such judgments to a Higher Power.

American Bandstand

In '59 a kind soul donated a television set
to the Convent. The nuns, unsure of the
gift, decided obedient postulants could watch

an hour each week. We argued over what we'd
watch that precious hour. Clicked through the three
available channels and found *American Bandstand*.

Girls and boys dancing, close dancing, fancy
dances. We felt the pull from Holy thoughts.
The boys had pompadours, the girls "big" hair.

 We chose boys we liked from the Bandstand
crowd. We talked about Bobby Rydell, Paul Anka
and our hearts beat faster when Dick Clark spoke.

They did the Stroll. We practiced the steps and
nailed it. After lights out, we'd hum the beat,
giggle and Stroll between our dorm beds. Our

bodies changed and when chaperoned outside
convent walls, to concerts or plays, whistles followed.

We weren't equipped to handle this attention.

Prayers were redirected. After Bandstand's sacred
hour we drifted to the second-floor porch. Higher than
the Convent walls, boys yowled beneath like tom-cats

with yells and whistles. For the first time we wore the
ill-fitting cloak of seduction. Lord knows we learned nothing

about sex or our bodies from the good Sisters. Were
the emotions I felt due to hormones, moon cycles?
Was it normal? Need I voice my sudden delight

in impure thoughts in the darkened
confessional? Would Father Mahoney
recognize my voice? Caught when we squealed

and made a ruckus, punishment followed. We
knelt in corners and prayed for forgiveness.
The Sisters struck our bare heels if our backs weren't

straight enough. It made us pause, but a fire was lit.
Mother Superior called for me. *"Child, I fear you
don't have a true calling. Pray on it, ask for God's*

intercession. If it's His will we'll take you in." I packed
my things and phoned home. I'd failed Mama,
but freedom tasted sweet upon my tongue.

Dark Stone

As contained as a box of fireworks,

imperceptible depths,

a dark side.

I loved his smooth olive skin,

his panther walk,

his sleek differences from high school beaus.

He was tight blue jeans, a slow wicked smile,

an unknown stirring in my genitals.

Alarms should have gone off.

My Mother's did.

A rough stone, no polished rock,

distilled white lightning—fatal to

a convent girl.

Violence bubbled,

flashed,

wounded.

Pain prayed on rosary beads.

His rock core allowed no admittance,

scarred by a mother with

too many men on her dance card.

Dirty Laundry

It's not the whitened circle from the ever-present can of
Copenhagen
       worn into the fabric of the right back pocket,
       smoke rings blown towards a Gibbous moon.
It's not the leather belt I remove with its hefty
       silver buckle that resides beneath his umbilicus.
It's not when they're on a heap on the bedroom floor,

It is when they assume his shape, when those long legs climb
into them, take on that swagger.
It's the blueprint created by many wearings and washings that
hide and reveal
the workings of the body I crave, the fly curving around his
penis,
       weighty, whitened, frayed.
It's when I hold the jeans to my face, inhale wood smoke, the
musky
       male smell that is his alone, a pungent intoxicant that
stirs my senses.
It's when I touch the soft cotton, so like caressing his bare
skin that I want to howl.

A tendril of white string, intimately trundled to my groin, has unraveled from its hem

      and tickles my nose as I release them into the wash water.

Leaving Normal

At eighteen, I married
a man I barely knew.
Teen hormones ignited
passion. Betrayed by lust
I turned the knob
and the door swung wide,
away from family hugs,
and kisses. Learned to lie
about bruises and broken
bones. Learned to say I'd
fallen and *Oh, I'm fine.*
Learned to wear long sleeves
and smile while pain
curled me into my shell.
Was taught not to believe the myth
of happily ever after. When I did
confess, the priest said,
divorce was not an option.
He said I must lie in the blessed bed
the Catholic Church had fashioned.
I studied the blueprint of my parents'
mating, my grandparents' 55 years

of courting. Fueled by Jim Beam,

my husband screamed,

It's your fault that I hit you.

His words left me ashamed

I could still love him.

His violence, my fear,

became the paint upon our walls,

until his rage

turned toward our daughter.

I soothed her cries, shut that door,

and she and I searched for normal.

moving on

Echo Boy

She kneels on the last plank of the dock,
the early evening sky casts
light and shadow across her face.

She cups her hands around her mouth
and calls out – *Echo Boy*, as loud as she
can muster. Across the lake, beyond the beaver

pond, comes an answer – *Echo Boy*,
Echo Boy, Echo Boy like ripples
on the water.

She holds a hand to her ear
to fathom the mystery wrought
by sound over wind and water.

She's still there on the edge
at violet dusk. The water calm,
the night still. She calls out again.

Echo Boy, I'm here.
I'm here, I'm here, I'm here,
he answers.

A Field Guide

I walk into the woods,
to a world of hemlock, spruce,

and fir. Add gifts of cedar and juniper.
The scent of pine arouses me.

Beneath snow-burdened branches I stand.
Blankets of needles, cones cushion

my feet. Their hush and height
and patch of sky are my church.

Birch stands accent varied shades
of gray. Slender companions, white-robed nuns

who chant and sway. The wind between
the trees take up their cry. I hear the clunk

and click of ice unmoored from river's
edge by winter currents. The only human stains

are my way in. But I am not alone. Finches
skitter from branch to branch. Chippies

frolic in the snow. Icicles glitter overhead,
open their dripping mouths to speak.

Above an eagle dips a wing
in benediction to this day.

Blueberry Picking

Just days past summer solstice, I push my son's
buggy down the winding path.
Beneath the mosquito netting, he's soothed to sleep
by the tinny lullaby of buckets clinking together.

Gnats gnaw on the sweat at the back of my neck,
rosy sunburn grows fierce
in the shimmer of midday sun.

When I stop to pick, ants
climb the towers of my freckled legs.
I brush at them, but they track
my blue-veined highways.

I pick my fill. Close my eyes against the heat
and hundreds of blueberry eyes stare back at me.
Purple juice stains my fingers, saturates the oval
of my mouth.

Heavy-bottomed bees hover over the space
we share, land like tiny helicopters on
the dense bushes, sample sweet liquid

before they move on to a fresh patch.

My baby turns in his sleep, jiggles the cans.

Startled by the clanking, his hands splay,

brown eyes open, and he smiles.

Grede Foundry's Nurse

Through the eye of the magnifying lens, she
absorbs the swirls, whorls, tunnels worn

into his fingers, discovers the splinter
driven deep beneath his black-ridged nail,

the angle of his hand in hers, the measured beat
of his pulse. The tweezers grasp and free the wedge

of rotted wood, blood bubbles in the newly absented space,
spills over. They are pleased it is gone. She submerges

his hand into a basin of warm water, his body relaxes,
the metallic smell of the smoky foundry

seeps from his sweaty tee shirt, a momentary reprieve
in a grueling gray shift.

The Ringmaster

Because I know the fat lady's heart
is breakable, I cheer her cheerless
chores. I ice bruises and mend injuries.
When she cries I hand out Kleenex.
I know her weight by stone. Social Services
want to know who taught her son to call
his teachers' dildos. Her mind repeats
the same song over and over. I know she
measures herself against her 90-pound
daughter – bent beneath the weight of her
lover. It's driving her around the bend,
images of her man and this child she carried.
I phone when she's a no-show, log absences
as excused. I ask the union to dicker,
to defend her job to management. In jobs
where muscle counts, women make up the
weaker ten-percent. Men can be cruel. It's not
easy to be the brunt of jokes. Beneath jeans
and worn-out tees, her bras and panties
sparkle like jewels. She paints her lips,
wears perfume, can't seem to catch a break.

Beecher, Wisconsin

They say the fried chicken served for dinner
at Mary's Place makes Sunday worthwhile.
My hubby hums, "Drive by Mary's Place"
each time we hit the town limits. But, we don't
drive by, we pull on in. We sit at oilcloth-covered
tables, the pattern rubbed down to white slick.
Your bare elbow gets gummy if you lean on it.

There's been a For Sale sign out front
for the last six years. Bessie, our waitress,
doesn't bother with the hard sell she gives
strangers. She knows what we'll order.
The Faith Baptist Church crowd
are hungry after the long service.
You can tell the mood of the sermon

by their happy or solemn faces, by the pile
of chicken bones left on the plates.
Most local kids are home-schooled.
No shaved heads. No Goth. No piercings.
World events are discussed by truckers.
US141 runs dab-smack through Beecher's

middle. Townspeople stick to gossip,

 weddings or deaths, and who's been arrested.
The bus boy, Mary's nephew Hughie, has Down's
and a smile like a lit jukebox. He wears
his favorite Packer tee shirt, waves a big Hi.

We're sitting behind two guys in
double breasted suits. They're Beecher
butchers and they're bitching that college
kids stole their new sign last night—
Beecher Meat. My hubby glues my hand
to the sticky oilcloth to stifle my giggle.

The Mating of Loons

Praise the constancy of these black-billed birds –
their piercing cries carry over fog

before dawn breaks. Echoes from the far channel,
a distant aria, as if another wedded pair

have come to nest. They circle, dive, feed.
Each searches for the other when their

winged bodies slice the silver of the lake.
In slow concentric patterns, they waltz and talk,

flutter feathers of deepest snow and night,
Wear tribal bands about their necks,

true partners in this sacred place.

Traveling

Train windows offer

a world through panes of glass;

chug to Ile St. Louis,

Istanbul, or Marrakesh.

Fires set to pyres piled

with marigolds,

like pyramids of coins.

Taste ripe berries in

Tuscan wine with bourgeois stew

and crusty bread.

Above a roofless church a cappella

hymns ascend.

The Road In

I edge off M-95 onto the gravel road,
set my teeth to the jaw-jarring of tires
from the washboard left by too many lumber trucks.
ABBA is blaring. My head is full of alliteration,
assonance, and resonant verbs, detritus from Poetry class.

My eyes follow a hawk overhead, on
the two-rut road, gouged with potholes.
Distracted from *Fernando's* heavy drumbeat,
I watch for hidden rocks and pause passing
Big Bend Camp, taking pleasure in the hug

of the curve of the Michigamme.
Afternoon sun flickers off the water.
Currents eddy around deadhead logs
and up-heaved sandbars. Change its pace.

Slow it down. Recharged, it moves rapidly,
finds momentum. Where the road's
widened by loggers, I pushed my
son's buggy. On hot summer days

he'd sleep, lulled by buckets bumping
together. I plucked and ate wild blueberries,
juice staining my mouth, my fingers.
Berries no longer grow there. Beyond

the absent berry bushes, lush hardwoods
are erased. Shaking aspens, virgin maples,
and oaks are gone. Larches, red pines,

and scrub trees remain –shoddy substitutes.
The forest seems shamed. Fiddlehead ferns
curl and brown. I round the corner by Eckloff's
camp. At the last turn I see loons circling
as I park between the birches.

Laws of Nature

Geese are noisy birds. The laws of nature should control their

hoarse, pre-dawn discussions from the observation deck on

Crystal Lake.

Nature has no interest in my getting a good-night's sleep.

The migrants honk on about their sunny winter destinations.

I burrow my sleep-starved face in the pillow, think of the icy

winter ahead,

try to navigate the road back to REM.

To the East, a Chicago-Northwestern freight train blows its

whistle,

a sound of loss, traveling blind through town after town.

A nano-second of sleep and I'm

on the train,

ancient windows frame the gothic bridges in Prague,

click like a slideshow behind shuttered eyes,

down the Dalmatian coast, past Romanian farms,

to the clatter of wheels on silver rails, moving

out of earshot, going somewhere, everywhere,

a faint far-off, final whistle.

The spoor of skunk slinks behind my hydrangeas.

The dog across the alley catches scent, yaps frenziedly.

Covens of mourning doves walk electrical lines

like Cirque du Soleil performers, mutter and coo

incantations. Two doors down, our neighbor guns

his rebuilt Harley, tears down Cook Street

to his minimum wage job. The geese circle,

honk over the house. Incessant pounding

sets in, an early morning repair job

that pins me to the pillow with each

hammer blow. I shut my alarm off

before it rings.

Neither Earth nor Sky

Day leaks through slits of shades.
In shadowy light a moth quivers
on the wall. Your beard scrapes
while your lips pin me to the pillow

case. Our limbs tangle in the sheets.
You part my knees, our hips bang,
cymbals celebrating song. Smells of moist
and musk envelope us. Your tongue

rings round my ear, I hear you whisper
my name – Holy, Holy. The moth still
quivers on the wall. Our toes dig in,
bodies turn like a carousel in the dark.

We ride the tides of lunar madness,
gallop onward at lust's command.
Catch a brass ring, cross the chasm.
My lips taste the salt of distant rivers.
without need for speech or song.

After You're Gone

After you're gone, I'll forget why we bickered,
our differences, angers, complaints.
I'll remember goodnight kisses,

and early morning loving, laughter and hugs.
After you're gone,
I'll bury my face in the sleeve

of your favorite flannel shirt,
breathe in the scent that clings to the cotton.
After you're gone

I'll look for you on every street,
in each passing car. I'll search for
your walk, the back of your head.

I'll listen for your voice in each conversation.
After you're gone,
I'll hoard up stories to share,

store up caresses, remember your warmth
on cold winter nights, my body chilled
by your absence.

Over the years, when I've traveled
to far-away places, you were my home
at journey's end. After I'm gone,

in that moment between living and dying,
when we seek one human connection,
you'll be the home I'll travel to.

slices of life

Shall Not Hurt Them

I was seven when I laid hands on Missy Milburn's head
and stopped her fits. I felt the Spirit working
through me and her twitching ceased.

I learned about the healing of herbs, and found
them in creek beds, in dried blossoms, discovered
that spider webs can halt bleeding that

stinging nettles may be brewed into teas
and yellow yarrow works as a poultice and such.
I started handling serpents on my own.

Timber rattlers, cottonmouths, mostly.
Love the shift of their skin, the sleep of them
sunning on warm rocks,

like babies in the cradle of the gunnysack.
Unwinding out of darkness they coil around me,
like the arms of a mother scared to lose her child.

There's holiness there.

Mama took sick. I nursed her three
days and three nights, dosed her with
coneflower and hyssop for fever. Tried

wormwood tinctures that should have eased
her retching. Even used leeches from the creek
to bleed her though those black barnacles with,

their ooze of blood clinging to her white
skin made me puke. I fell asleep the fourth
morning. When I woke she'd passed. I am a healer who
couldn't heal her own Mama.

It was a month before my thirteenth birthday.

Now, on nights when the moon's
riding high and Pa's got a skinful

of shine, he comes looking for me.
I keep a gunnysack full of snakes
by my bed. He catches sight

of the brown burlap moving
like a giant muscle and he finds
elsewhere to lie.

On Many a Dark Night

Dusk is shrouded, night a fevered wish.
I bury my mojo beneath a conjurer's rock.
My bloated belly stares at an empty dish.
I weep because black magic can't stop this futile clock.

Blue lightning zips, rips, cleaves open stone sky,
loses chase, spreads my soul over Daddy's field.
Leave the big house to the buzz of a bluebottle fly,
whisper over my baby's grave, *Let escape be revealed.*

Feel the earth through my bare toes, bleed open my mind,
know there is no safe place to hide.
Pursued by death, I'm sure that they'll find

my body's bones before the moon is too bright.
Freedom's a forgotten wish, a place inclined
to exist beyond my reach as I run through the night.

Float Unrooted

Condoms float to the top, buoyant as fish bladders.
A beer can tumbles in the turgid waters, filling and emptying
with the tides, sending a blind silver eye skyward again and

again. Floating sea grasses grasp a slender ankle. The corpse
spins, draws back, shrugs one naked shoulder in a watery
tango. Tiny fish have eaten her eyes leaving dark, empty holes

to peer silently back, keeping her secrets. A thin line of
broken vessels encircle her neck like a blue agate necklace
worn by an elegant debutante. She's nestled among discarded
debris

from sunken ships; old anchors, motors, fishing lines and
nets. The ancient iron and metal wear a green patina of
crustacean rust oxidation. Once they were treasures among
the hills and

the valleys of the river bed and its constant motion. I take a
last drag on my cigarette, toss it skyward, and watch the
lighted

tip spiral around and around, extinguishing itself as it hits the water.

Uncoupling

Daddy left one Sunday
morning for bagels. Mama
held open auditions for his
side of the bed. Enough men
to string around the Christmas tree

in Rockefeller Center.
I never believed the Grimm
tale of a Princess walking on razors
for the man she loved.
I believed in banging for pleasure.

We hooked up in Florence after
too many glasses of grappa.
For two weeks we hunkered down
in a pensione. My naked foot
in your bare-ass lap as you

painted my toes. I watched your
fly-catching mouth as you slept.
I felt your heavy hand on the
curve of my belly, the slack sleep

of your penis when sated. I close

my eyes and see your pulse
quiver as you lean your head on me.
My mind returns to those moments.
Something's shifted and now, I feel
love is possible. Even for unbelievers.

La Piscina

I tread water in this Olympic stretch of pool,

the water delicious in the afternoon heat –

a mere 10 degrees from the equator.

The baked blue tiles at its bottom shimmer –

their checkerboard scored by a grid

of white grout,

wavers to the water's surface,

wriggles into the saw-tooth pattern

of rick-rack sewn on my mother's kitchen

curtains, circa 1958. Halos of rainbows

rumba where the sun blesses

the ripples, slide into an intricate dance

as I move from one end to the other,

my legs ghostly white, disembodied

Ta – Thanks

Ta—to Mary Katherine O'Malley, the storekeeper on the
long, unpaved road from northeast Belfast to Donegal, who
herded me into a rickety sedan on a down-pouring day, drove
me miles and miles out of her way to a hostel managed by
elderly old maids. She regaled me with, "Ireland would be
a wonderful country if it only had a bit of roof on it and that's
the reason there's so many redheads', tis the rust!"

Ta—to Katy Margaret O'Neil from the backwash of
Connemara, who married her dully handsome first cousin,
who has since gone to fat and rotten teeth. She loves him and
their four idiot sons, whose noses and drool she wipes,
coaxing smiles from their vacant minds, counting them her
treasures.

Ta—to Granny Cassandra Mellon –the oldest living female in
Shannon, because she's nearing 90, she's given gifts of glass
after glass of Guiness. Her immense bulk overflows the chair
as she sips, knowing a body can live on Guinness as long as
you remember to eat a bit of cabbage now and then.

Ta— to Annie Kelso MacAfee, a slovenly housekeeper who's
newly inherited a run-down mansion in Galway and opened a

B&B, but alas, there's no breakfast as the milk curdles on the stoop, the cats roam the cupboards, and rusted plumbing rests in the stained tub on the second floor.

Ta— to Valerie Annie Peltham, a Belfast housewife, who grew up in the Cyprus sun, fell in love with David Peltham, an Irish minstrel with wandering eyes and a smile to break your heart. She gave birth to their daughter, Zoë, alone after thirty-two hours of labor, her narrow shut down face lined with dissatisfaction for both weather and wandering.

Ta -- to Brigit Murphy McPherson, a barmaid in County Clare, with a mustache and a wart on her nose, but whose singing of *Waltzing Matilda* sends chills down one's spine. Who was judged a "Good Craic" by the lads in McPherson's Pub, for any man in need of a glass.

Past Forgetting

She's in the john for the fourth time

this morning.

I measure out five sheets of Charmin

so the toilet won't plug.

The Crest is hidden.

She brushes

morning and night

but uses a squeeze

that would sparkle the teeth

of a family of eight.

Alone in the bathroom she believes

no one can hear her.

She talks to God and his Angel

about failures and sins that never took place.

Some days her mind is a gray slate lake

with no words to guide her.

She struggles into underpants, rolls

and unrolls the same pair of socks.

Worn out she hunts for the rest of her

clothes.

Her address book is buried deep in the snow.

Some days are blessed. She smiles,

becomes the *she*

before thinking failed.

Some days her mind works with the tides,

erases the remnants of memory not eaten

by a Great White with shiny, sharp teeth.

Last Dance

They sashay a slow waltz in wheelchairs and walkers
to the music of rubber-soled nurses and the clang
of bedpans. Their harmony is sneezes and wheezes
and snatches of forgotten songs. They drive their wheelchairs
over the threshold, their cart and their plow
over the bones of the dead.

Hours of waiting no clock can measure. They
no longer recognize their face in the mirror.
Served three meals as tasty as dog food,
they crave dessert, anything chocolate,
and eat it first.

They mourn children and grandchildren
who rarely visit, shuffle faded photos
with bent edges like collections of worn
baseball cards. No one collects baseball cards
anymore. Once they were craftsmen or artists

skilled at their jobs, now their hands shake
and their vision's blurred. Their hearing is
shot and they'd give all they owned

to share a few words with people they've loved.

The gift of a hug, a bright ribbon, or a few minutes
to listen to over-told tales, to see if they're happy, sad,
or confused. That is more important than charting
the body's decline or the mind's failure.
When they no longer speak and curl
into the womb,
when memory flies to the moon,
they'll go home
and their hours of waiting will end.

Chagall Dreams

She burrows into the pillow,
turns on the T.V. at three a.m.
and surfs for *me* time. She cares
for a 55-year-old Down's with
early dementia –who's forgotten

how to dress herself, who
can't wipe herself, who gets
stuck on the stairs and cries
she does not know how to go
up or down– who now sleeps

and travels through a night peopled
with blue cows and floating churches
and no vocabulary to explain any of it.
Life doesn't turn out the way you expect
it to. Her day will be spent looking after

and for things. The car keys are warming
in the oven. The list of lost things grows daily.
The sister no longer knows their brother's
face. She stuffs her pockets with broken treasures,

old envelopes, torn photos; this month's gas bill

is crumpled there. She's forgotten how to tell time.
They go to Mass where one evokes a novena
to an unlistening God, bargains, pleads
that for a little longer this child

she never birthed will not forget her name.
The other croons gibberish,
sings the chorus of *Oklahoma* during
the hymn, nibbles the host
like an hors-d'oeuvre, and hugs half
the parishioners after communion.

The sister falls asleep in the blue beanbag
chair watching reruns of *Little House*
on the Prairie as an ocean of wheat
drowns the smiling girl.

Turkeys in the Snow

Vulture kin,
beaks pecking
like a third leg on a balance beam.
They move through the corn-shorn snow.

A cacophony of noise marks their
trail as they search and savor
frozen kernels hiding in vanilla
snow.

Reptilian, obsidian-eyed.
Cold as black ice, unfeeling, uncaring.
Scavengers eking out their livelihood.
Wattles waving to their hungry, hurried beat.

Turkeys in the snow, moving on talon-tipped toes,
masticating, pebbles of fodder
moving rhythmically down
wrinkled goose-fleshed necks.

Featherless as plucked skeletons
above winged clutched coats.
Sentinels in the field –
metronome-bobbing heads

babbling and chanting to
grain-giving Earth Gods.
Turkeys in the snow.

Pity Party

I'm gonna' tell you this world makes it
hard to be different, to go around sporting
a blue wheelchair sign. I dislike stares
that don't count me as normal. I wear a hose
in my nose 'cause my lungs really suck.

Within each a snowstorm battles, while
the body they live in weakens and wanes.
I'm more than what's not working
inside me. I pull a can of oxygen behind me
like a dead dog. Children point and whisper,

"Mama, what's wrong with that lady?" I hear
the Calliope. The Carousel's a whirl and I'm Star
of the Big Top. A circus experience, I'm
a Geek in the making. It doesn't matter that I
wear lipstick, take care with my clothes.

It doesn't count that I smile and I'm pleasant,
unlike many who walk in my world. More often
than not I'm disregarded, seen but invisible,
not someone of worth. It doesn't matter that I'm
educated or that I've traveled the world. What

they see is not the *Who* that's me. People see me

lugging groceries, tipping my oxygen into a cart.
I see pity in their faces, but their pity's the last thing
I want. I'm still the *Me* that's hidden from sight.

I'm funny and smart. I've been desired, wedded
and bedded. Now, I'm seen as damaged,
less than someone who's whole.

Say When

When is it time to say enough is enough?
When do I say I'm going to lie back, not
struggle against odds that I cannot fight?
When do I stop trying new meds or a doctor
with new advice? For all of my life I've struggled
to breathe, an act that is natural for most human
beings. When do I let go and float on
without struggle and smile into sleep?
When do I say *When* and simply give up?

Fishing for Words

I cast a net upon a river of words,
pull them toward my boat,
repeat the casting, the pulling,
until the hold is full. I row
against currents that eddy like
a dark kite, until held captive

by its bank. I scatter my catch.
Shimmering words, flipping, flopping.
The blood red gills of their breath
open and close like scarlet umbrellas.
Pick me. Choose me. And I do.
I arrange the words into stories,

poems, precious, and painful memories.
Arrange. Rearrange.
Seek an ordained place for each,
use the fragments to make a whole.
Some words – wounded, unacceptable,
I return to the river for another day,
a separate purpose.

I am caught in the rhythm of words
and water along the curve of the stream.

Dunes of sandbars and deadhead logs
alter its pace, slow it down
until recharged it finds momentum,
rages into rapids.

I toil through the long twilight
until the face of the moon
arches high in the blue-black sky,
illuminating sentences.
I close my eyes,
say, It is good,
and sleep.

Dear Reader

Dear Reader,

What is it you look for in my writing? Something to fill you up, to repair the broken pieces within you? Or something to remove or delete sadness or emptiness inside you?

No one can do that for you, Reader. It is a task that is yours alone. We are our worse judge, our cruelest critic. Our vilest jury is made up of those we hold most dear.

It's hard to fathom but it is true. We look in stores, at ads on-line, on the screens of movies and television, in books for that which will smooth out our rough edges, plane away the knots and swirls in the uneven boards of our being.

We plead with the saints, archangels, even the demons of our existence to show us the path, the way out of the dark hole we are trapped in –making up prayers until there is no moisture in our dry mouths, our skin as chaffed as if rubbed by emery board. The same tune, a funeral dirge plays over and over until our heart beats to its rhythm; ka . . . thud, ka. . . thud, ka . . . thud . . . slower and slower . . . ka . . . thud, ka . . . thud, ka . . .

Thud, until it is but a single echo in an empty room. Don't ask too much of me, don't ask what I'm unable to give.

Dear Reader, The record skips. *Dear. Dear. Dear. Read. Read . . . er, Dear rea . . . der. Dear . . . read . . . er. D . . e . . a . . . r.*

Notes:

"drive their cart and their plow over the bones of the dead," in the poem: "Last Dance" is from William Blake's *Proverbs of Hell.'*

"Shall Not Hurt Them" is from a dream and from a quote in King James Bible: Mark 16:18

"They shall; take up serpents; and if they drink any deadly thing, it shall not hurt them; they shall lay hands on the sick, and they shall recover."